DRUGS AND CRIME

In South America, drug lords like Pablo Escobar became extremely powerful because of the large quantities of drugs they control.

THE DRUG ABUSE PREVENTION LIBRARY

DRUGS AND CRIME

Victor Adint

THE ROSEN PUBLISHING GROUP, INC.

NEW YORK

The people pictured in this book are only models. They in no way practice or endorse the activities illustrated. Captions serve only to explain the subjects of photographs and do not in any way imply a connection between the real-life models and the staged situations.

Published in 1994, 1997 by the Rosen Publishing Group, Inc.
29 East 21st Street, New York, NY 10010

Revised Edition 1997

Manufactured in the United States of America

Library of Congress Cataloging-in-Publication Data

Adint, Victor.
  Drugs and crime / Victor Adint.
    p.   cm. — (The Drug abuse prevention library)
  Includes bibliographical references and index.
  ISBN 0-8239-2604-4
    1. Drug abuse and crime—United States—Juvenile literature.
    2. Drug abuse—United States—Prevention—Juvenile literature.
    3. Youth—United States—Drug use—Juvenile literature. [Drug
    abuse.] I. Title. II. Series.
  HV5825.A665 1994
  364.2′4—dc20
                                                93-41862
                                                  CIP
                                                        AC

Contents

Introduction

Many teens are living in communities and going to schools where illegal drugs are becoming more and more common. Young people must make important choices about getting involved with drug dealing and other drug-related crimes.

Too often, people start using or dealing drugs without understanding all of the dangers. This book will tell you what you need to know about drugs and the drug business so you can make the best decisions for you.

Selling drugs may seem like an easy way to make money. Or, you may be told that using drugs will help you to escape your problems. But people who pressure you into selling or using illegal drugs won't tell you about all of the risks. The drug business is much more dangerous than it appears. This book will explain

the risks people take when they become
part of the drug trade.

By definition, street drugs and crime
go together. Buying, selling, or
possessing any street drug (including
marijuana, cocaine, and heroin) is
against the law. Each of these crimes can
get you arrested and fined or put in jail.

In addition, people often break other
laws to buy, sell, or use drugs. Every
year, thousands of people are arrested,
hurt, or killed in drug-related crimes.

This book will tell you how the drug
business works, from the buyer to the
seller to the drug lord who runs the
business. It will tell you how teens get
involved in the drug trade and the
dangers they face. Finally, it will give you
the information you need to help you
make educated decisions.

CHAPTER 1

The Definition of Drugs

*T*here are two ways that drugs are sold: at licensed pharmacies and on the streets.

Medicines

Licensed pharmacies sell medicines to treat, prevent, or cure diseases. There are two kinds of medicines: prescription drugs and over-the-counter drugs.

Prescription drugs are medicines that only pharmacists can legally sell. They can be sold only to people who have had a doctor prescribe the proper dosage and strength.

Over-the-counter drugs can be bought without a doctor's prescription. These drugs include aspirin, cough syrup, and vitamins.

Prescription and over-the-counter drugs are legal. They are made in regulated laboratories. Doctors, pharmacologists, and the U.S. government make

Most of the illegal drugs sold on the street are prepared in kitchens, bathrooms, or abandoned buildings.

10 sure these drugs are tested and proven safe and effective.

However, prescription drugs are sometimes sold illegally on the street. Dealers often tamper with these drugs. And even if they are not tampered with, the drugs can be harmful if they have not been prescribed by a doctor.

Street Drugs

Street drugs, such as marijuana, cocaine, heroin, d-lysergic acid (LSD), and phencyclidine (PCP), are illegal in the U.S. These drugs are often made in laboratories that do not have safety standards. The people who run these labs are called "chemists." Those who make the drugs are called "cooks."

Unlike pharmacists, who learn mixing techniques, drug cooks combine dangerous chemicals with no regard for safety. Instead, they try to make powerful drugs that will sell well on the streets. When cooks make a bad batch of a drug, they often sell it anyway. Many people have died from taking such drugs.

Cocaine and Crack

Cocaine comes from the coca leaf. The leaves are mixed with kerosene, acetone, or gasoline, then soaked and mashed into a paste. The paste is refined into cocaine.

Cocaine can be smoked, snorted, or injected. But first, a drug dealer may dilute (known as "cutting" or "hitting") the raw cocaine with other substances such as sugars or local anesthetics. By increasing the bulk and decreasing the potency, a dealer can maximize his or her own profit.

Crack is made from cocaine hydrochloride and baking soda. The result is a solid "rock" of cocaine that can be smoked. Cocaine, especially in the form of crack, is highly addictive.

Heroin

On the street, heroin is called "horse," "smack," and "Mexican brown." Heroin is made from the seed pod of the poppy plant. It is often cut with powdered milk, sugar, or starch. People can snort or inject the drug. Heroin is highly addictive.

Recently, the popularity of heroin has increased dramatically. In 1995, the rate of high school seniors who used heroin surpassed any previous year. This may be because heroin is cheaper and more potent than ever before. Today, the number of heroin users is up to 2 million.

12 | *Hallucinogens*

Hallucinogens are drugs that make a person see and hear things that aren't real. LSD, or "acid," and PCP, or "angel dust," are two such drugs.

Marijuana, or "pot," comes from the leaves of the cannabis or hemp plant. Tetrahydrocannabinol, or THC, is the chemical that creates a high when marijuana is smoked. Drugs such as PCP, hashish oil, and cocaine, are often added to make marijuana more powerful.

Amphetamines

Amphetamines and methamphetamines are stimulants known as "meth," "crank," "speed," and "ice." They can dangerously speed up your heart rate and can cause hallucinations. Most amphetamines are taken as pills. But ice is a crystal form that is smoked. MDMA, or Ecstasy, is made from amphetamines.

Drug users put their lives in the hands of the drug dealer, the chemist, the cook, and all the other people who handled the drug. Are you prepared to trust these people with your life? Or, as a drug dealer, are you willing to take responsibility for someone else's life?

CHAPTER 2

The Business of Drugs

*L*ike any other business, the drug business has a hierarchy.

A small circle of drug lords rule from the top. They make the most money and take the fewest risks in the drug business.

People in the middle import the drugs from other countries. They arrange to have the drugs cut and then distributed to dealers. The drug lords trust only a few people to do this. Most lower-level people get killed or go to jail before they can reach this level.

The largest number of people in the drug business are the dealers at the bottom. These people take most of the risks and are the most likely to be killed. This is the level at which teens are recruited to join the business.

14 | *Heroin, Cocaine, and Marijuana*

Drug lords live in other countries where they grow, harvest, and process cocaine, heroin, and marijuana in large quantities. Drugs are big business, and the money the drug lords make buys them a lot of power. They hire their own armies and pay off government officials. The United States Drug Enforcement Agency cannot arrest them unless their government cooperates or they come into the United States.

Drug lords use local people to harvest and process the drugs. Many of these people are paid with crude forms of the drugs or with by-products (waste). Many workers who process cocaine are paid with cocaine paste.

The drugs are shipped to the United States and received by middle-level drug smugglers. These smugglers are usually "family." Their job is to sell the drugs to distributors. The distributor cuts the drug and sells or fronts it to several dealers. Fronting is like wholesaling. When a drug is fronted to a distributor, a price is agreed upon and the distributor has to come up with the money later. If he fails to come up with the money, family or not, he is punished or killed. *There is always some-one to take his place.*

Thousands of lives are lost every year because of drug-related crime.

16   The distributor then tests the drug for strength and cuts it again. "Pigs" are often used to test the drugs. Pigs are people who want to get into the business. They are told that taking the drug is part of their initiation. Many of them do not survive the initiation. The drug is then sold or fronted to dealers who control certain city or rural areas. The drug is tested again and cut. The dealers then recruit gangs or street dealers to sell the drug to the users.

Street dealers or gangs who work for dealers are fronted drugs to sell. They are required to sell the drugs and return the money to the dealer running their area. Street dealers are usually given a small amount of the drug to sell for their own profit. Street dealers end up in jail, addicted to drugs, or dead more frequently than anybody else in the drug business. The ones who become addicted are not trusted by those higher in the ranks and often end up dead. The chances for a street dealer to advance and become a low-level distributor are almost zero. Street dealers know this, and it adds to the pressure of doing their job. All they care about is selling the drugs and improving their chances of promotion.

Police in Colombia, South America, spray fields of poppies with chemicals to destroy the crop.

One person's choice to use drugs can affect many innocent
people. This subway car derailed because the conductor was
under the influence of drugs.

There are two ways a street dealer can move up in the business. One is to outlive and replace someone higher up. The other is to buy drugs in large quantities and start his or her own operation. A dealer who chooses this path is almost immediately marked for death by other dealers and street gangs. Competition in the drug business is not appreciated or encouraged.

Made in the USA

Drugs such as LSD, PCP, Ecstasy, and amphetamines, are usually made in the United States. They are made in small illegal labs or factories. The business of selling these drugs is much smaller than for imported drugs such as heroin, cocaine, and marijuana.

Once the drugs are made and tested, they are packaged and sold to the distributors or dealers. After buying the drugs, dealers will sell them on the streets.

In the past, the police have had a hard time locating and shutting down these small operations. In 1987, a branch of the U.S. Department of Justice provided funds to develop the Clandestine Laboratory Enforcement Program (CLEP). CLEP is a national program that trains law officials to find and safely shut down the

20 illegal drug labs. The program has been very successful. Law enforcement agencies across the country have become better prepared to find and close down local drug labs.

Laundering Money

Because drug activity is illegal in the U.S., money made from drug transactions must be spent carefully.

To avoid prosecution, drug lords "launder" their money. This means that they hide it from the government in various ways.

Some high-level drug dealers set up legal businesses, such as retail stores, so they can claim their drug money as legal income. They pretend that the drug money came from the business. Then it is taxed along with the legal money from the business, and they can spend it.

According to federal laws, any property owned by a drug dealer can be seized by the government if the government can prove that it was paid for or partly paid for with drug money. Drug dealers who don't have a way to launder their money can't spend it easily. They keep large amounts of cash around and hope they will be able to find a way to spend it without attracting the attention of the police.

It may be tempting for some teens to accept drugs from friends, but it is wiser to say no.

The U.S. Drug Enforcement Agency seizes tons of illegally imported drugs every year.

Drug-Related Crime

Since drug users and dealers are already criminals, most of them have no problem committing other crimes. It has been estimated that drug users are four to six times more likely than others to commit other crimes. There are many crimes that are common among drug users and dealers.

Theft—Some drug addicts don't have the money to pay for drugs. So they rob houses and stores and trade the stolen property for drugs. Drug dealers accept the stolen merchandise as payment. A $500 TV can be sold to a dealer for $50 worth of drugs—10 percent of its market value. The dealer can then resell the stolen TV on the street for 50 to 70 percent of its worth. The dealer gets $250 to $350 for fifty dollars worth of drugs.

Gun Violence—Gun violence is often connected to the drug business. According to a 1993 report, 60 percent of drug dealers carry a gun when they are selling drugs. Communities that have had a rise in the number of people or gangs trying to sell drugs have also had an increase in the number of murders.

24   Drug dealers feel the need to protect themselves, especially from other dealers. As the number of teens selling drugs increases, so does the number of teens carrying guns. The number of murders, particularly those committed with guns, also rises.

Most of the guns used in the drug business are stolen or sold illegally. Adult dealers don't buy legal guns because they are easier for the police to trace. Teen drug dealers must buy guns illegally because it is against the law for anyone under eighteen to buy or carry firearms.

Prostitution—Dealers are often involved in prostitution. Some addicts sell their bodies for drugs. The drug dealer either trades drugs for sex with them, or sells the sex to someone else. Many young drug addicts, both boys and girls, end up as prostitutes.

People who trade sex for drugs are said to be "turned out." A girl who trades sex for drugs is often called a "strawberry." Someone who is turned out gets little or no respect in the drug business. He or she is often abused by the dealers as well as the people who buy sex from him or her.

As drug use has grown, street gangs have taken over much of the drug dealing that happens on city streets.

Illegal protection—Drug dealers can't go to the police if someone rips them off or if rivals threaten them. They often hire gang members to protect them. Or they can start their own gangs. Drug lords in other countries protect themselves by hiring or creating their own armies.

25

Drug-awareness programs have become an important part of our educational system.

CHAPTER 3

Drugs, Crime, and Youth

*T*he drug business requires people to take risks. No risk, no money. As the risk increases, the level of trust among people in the business decreases. Drug enforcement is getting tougher, and the sentences for drug crimes are longer. Dealers and gang members are less willing to do their own dirty work.

Adolescents are treated different by the law. The criminal justice system is much easier on them. Dealers would rather let teenagers "take the fall" (be arrested). A younger person is easier to scare and control. Dealers are less concerned about being double-crossed. Younger and younger boys and girls are being recruited $\quad$ **27**

28 into the business. Young people work as lookouts, spotters, couriers, dealers, enforcers, prostitutes, and pigs.

Lookouts do just that. They keep an eye on the street. If they see an unfamiliar face, they warn the dealer. They look for cops and rival dealers or gangs.

Spotters are usually used at the sales location. They don't sell the drug or possess it. Spotters direct drug users to an ideal place where they can buy drugs. The dealers might be on the roof of a building and use a piece of string and a can to exchange drugs for money. They may also use rooms that have access to the street. A dealer barricades any obvious entryways, keeps an open escape route, and makes a small opening in a wall or a barricaded door to pass drugs to and receive money from the users. If the police bust the operation, the dealer has a good chance of getting away. The spotter runs the highest risk of being arrested.

Couriers carry drugs around town. Who would suspect a 12-year-old boy or girl on a bicycle of carrying drugs? Most of the time the kids are not told what's in the bag and warned not to look. They're just given five or ten dollars and told to take it somewhere.

Young dealers sell drugs in small amounts to other kids. As they get older they may be trusted with larger amounts to sell.

Enforcers are generally gang members. Gangs are recruited or created to control certain areas. They keep out competition, increase the sales territory, collect debts, protect the dealer, and guard the operation from theft. Gang members are always highly visible and attract the attention of the police. They are also very expendable. They tend to last from one day to two years. Many of them end up physically hurt, in jail, addicted to drugs, or dead.

Young prostitutes are called "slaves" because they are owned by people in the business. They don't have a choice and can't say no. People who buy sex don't want to get AIDS. AIDS can be transmitted through sex and by sharing needles. Men and women who have been "pulling tricks" (prostituting) for a long time and who do drugs are more likely to have AIDS. Dealers believe that a young boy or girl is safer because he or she has had little or no sexual experience. Because of the danger of AIDS, more and more young boys and girls are being recruited into prostitution or slavery.

Everyone can get together to rally against drugs and crime in their neighborhood.

Teenagers at a Disadvantage

Most teenagers and parents survive growing up; most parents try to understand their children and accept them as unique individuals. They allow them more responsibility, and give them the love and support they need. However, many young people are unhappy with their lives. Growing up is not always easy, and some have it worse than others. Feeling misunderstood and wanting to rebel is a normal part of being young. To grow up, teenagers have to slowly move away from their parents and the control of other authority figures. They need to learn how to make their own decisions. When parents are unwilling to let their kids grow up, teenagers sometimes make poor decisions. These decisions are based on anger and rebellion. All teenagers are in danger of recruitment for drug activity when they are rebelling. Those from poorer homes have a harder time and find drugs and crime more attractive.

Young people who live in families where they are abused (physically or sexually) or neglected have it the hardest. They don't have a healthy support system to help them reach their goals in acceptable ways. Many young people who live in

Drug-free zones discourage dealers and gangs from selling drugs near schools.

inner-city areas or ghettos feel trapped. The idea of completing school and getting a good job may seem impossible. They may see the drug business as the only way out. Some of them decide that drugs may help them cope with their lives or that a gang may take the place of their family.

Recruitment

Drug dealers and gang members have no trouble finding recruits. Some young people jump at the chance to be involved. Others are tricked or forced into the business. Disadvantaged youths are the most vulnerable to recruiters.

Drugs can be very attractive. Just using them is rebellious. Teens may find that drugs give them temporary self-esteem and relief from emotional pain. Drugs seem to help at first, but they quickly turn against the users. Users become dependent on the drug and eventually addicted.

Soon drugs stop working as well as they used to, and the addicts need more to get relief. Then, when they can't afford the drugs, they will do just about anything to get them. Many addicts steal property, deal drugs, and sell their bodies to support their habit. They are looked down on by other people in the business.

34 | *Attraction*

Drug dealers recruit by attraction. People who see drugs as the only way to make money are easily drawn into the business. They start by getting to know a dealer and then do jobs like being a lookout, a spotter, a courier, and possibly a pig. If they survive this and do their jobs well, they are eventually trusted to deal drugs in small quantities. Young people who get involved in this way are in it for their own gain so they are more likely to cross the dealer. Dealers know this and try to keep them from being too successful. So long as the teenager needs the dealer, the dealer can control and use him or her.

Trickery

Drug dealers recruit by trickery. They befriend a teenage boy, for example, who seems vulnerable. They spend time with him, and give him money. The dealer wants the youth to turn against his parents and rely on him for emotional and physical needs. The dealer becomes a second parent and at first may do a better job than the real parents.

When the teenager feels obligated, the dealer asks him to do favors. Before too long, the teenager is carrying drugs, being a lookout, a spotter, or a pig, and dealing drugs to his friends. Dealers like to recruit this way because the youth does the favors out of gratitude and friendship. He is not out for personal gain, so he is less likely to cross the dealer. As the youth begins to realize that he is being used, the dealer regains control by getting him hooked on drugs and introducing him to prostitution.

Gang Recruiting

Gang leaders also recruit by attraction. Some teenagers have given up on school and getting a good job. They lack purpose and a feeling of importance. They may feel lost. Teenagers who lack a loving and understanding family feel a great deal of emptiness. Everybody needs something to work for and needs to feel important.

In the beginning, a gang can give a teenager a sense of purpose, importance, hope, and family unity. Later, the youth finds that the unity, loyalty, and love quickly dissolve. You don't make your own decisions in a gang. You're either in or out. You do what they want you to do, or you are rejected and punished. The gang's unity, loyalty, and love depend on your *obedience*; there is no freedom. Gang members are forced to do things that go

36 against their beliefs. A gang member has
to turn his back on himself.

People who want to be in gangs generally hang out with gang members. They
get in by doing favors. When they prove
that they are loyal or deserve respect, they
are accepted. To do that, they have to do
something that hurts them or puts them in
danger. They have to show that the gang
is more important than they are. This is
called "initiation." The gang won't trust
them unless they are willing to put the
gang's needs ahead of their own.

The Trap

The drug business becomes a trap for
many people who are drawn in by the idea
of money, power, freedom, and happiness.
Once they're in, many people realize that
the business is not what they expected.

Money can be made by dealing drugs.
The only problem is that it's a different
kind of money. Sure, it can buy nice
things, but at what cost? To make money
and survive, dealers and gang members
have to be meaner and crueler than the
next guy. A good dealer has to be able to
put business before everything else.

When most young people start out in
the business, they have a conscience, a

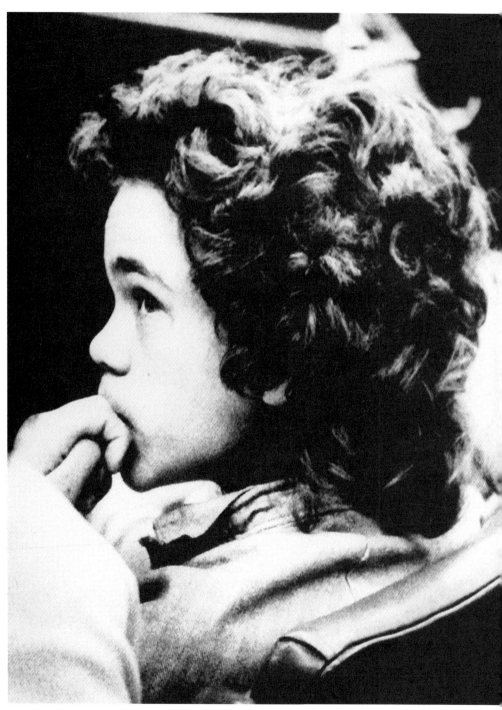

This 13-year-old boy was arrested on suspicion of dealing drugs.
The money that can be made dealing is attractive even to the very
young, but selling drugs can carry a heavy price if you're caught.

38 sense of right and wrong. Most of them believe that they will be different. They say, "If I don't do it, someone else will. Heck, I could make a lot of money and go legit. I won't do the things other dealers or gang members do. I won't cross my friends, sell drugs to younger kids, steal from my family or friends, hurt other people, or abuse drugs and become addicted. I won't take any foolish risks, and I won't get caught by the police." What most young people don't realize is that they have to do *all* those things and *more* to survive and make it in the business.

Young people are of great importance in the drug business. The law treats them differently, and the dealers take advantage of that. Most experienced dealers have a criminal record and face longer prison terms than youths under 16 or 18.

Getting Hooked on Money

In the beginning, the youth is asked to do light work. The work has little risk (compared to other tasks) and does not require him to go seriously against his values. If the youth performs well, he is paid. The money and acceptance are rewarding at first. But the teen quickly learns that the other people are making a lot more money.

This triggers an ambition to move up in the business. As the teen becomes more attracted to the money and power, he becomes more willing to do the things he swore he would never do.

The teen is then required to do dirtier work: collections, theft, violence, vandalism, and prostitution. The teen at first may be somewhat uncomfortable with these new tasks, but he is already trapped. By now the youth is addicted to the business and totally hooked on the money. He is afraid to disappoint the dealer or gang, and terrified of being rejected or thought of as not "cool." To continue in the business, the teen has to change all of his values and shut off his emotions. Feelings get in the way. They make him feel bad about what he's doing and less able to do what it takes to succeed and survive in the business. The youth must *isolate* himself from his feelings and ignore or change his values and morals.

Losing Trust and Friendship

As he moves up in the business, the teen learns that he can't trust anyone. Everyone wants to make more money and have more power. Teens are loyal to one another only if they can benefit from that

40 loyalty. If they believe that crossing someone will bring them more benefit than
harm, they'll do it. A successful dealer has
to make others fear him and believe that
they will benefit from working for him.

Friendships cease to matter. The youth
learns to isolate himself from others because he can't trust their friendship. He
can't trust anyone with his feelings and
thoughts because they might be used
against him. If he allows himself to care
about people in the business, he will be
hurt if they cross him or feel the pain of
loss if they are killed. He may even have
to kill his own friend out of duty to his
dealer or gang, or to gain more fear and
respect from his peers. Loved ones who
are not in the business are also a threat.
If a boss wants to punish him or make him
do something he doesn't want to do, the
boss goes after his friends and family.

If you think about it, the youth is already in jail. He has turned his back on
his own values, morals, and feelings. He
is isolated because he can't allow himself
close friendships. No matter how much
money he has, it's not enough. He con-
stantly has to make sure he isn't being
crossed. He also has to worry about being
caught by the police. If he spends his

Drug dependency will eventually ruin your life.

money carelessly, the government will bust him for tax evasion or seize his property.

A dealer who wants to get out of the business finds it almost impossible. People in the business don't like it when someone tries to go straight. They worry that he may talk to the police. If a dealer is making a profit for others, they might not allow the person to get out until he is no longer useful to them. *The money made in the business carries an enormous price.*

Depending on the judge, young people can either serve time in a juvenile facility or be placed in an institution with adult criminals.

CHAPTER 4

Busted

What happens when a person gets busted? Every juvenile court has broad authority when deciding how to punish teen offenders. Judges have flexibility when making decisions, and often give adolescents more opportunities for rehabilitation than adult courts do.

Although people will tell you otherwise, young people are not punished less severely than adults. They get less protection from the law. It's easier for a person under 18 to be convicted of a crime. Incarceration terms are based on the same penal codes used for adults.

Being a teen also doesn't protect you from having a permanent criminal record. Juvenile criminal files are not automatically sealed when an adolescent turns 18. A criminal record could affect your ability to get a job or a loan from a bank.

44 An adolescent has to ask the court to have his file sealed. If an adolescent continues to get in trouble with the law after the age of 18, his file remains open.

Different Courts

There are many differences between juvenile and adult courts. Unsupported testimony of an accomplice can be used against a minor. That means a police officer may not have to find someone to back up an accomplice's story. The story may be used against the adolescent in court. A juvenile can be arrested on a misdemeanor charge without a warrant, even if the officer didn't see the adolescent commit the crime and wasn't in the immediate area. If an adolescent commits a crime and gets away, an officer can arrest the adolescent if there is good reason to believe he committed the crime. To arrest an adult in the same situation, a police officer has to get permission from a judge (a warrant). Adolescents do not have a right to bail. If an adolescent is locked up, he is not permitted to pay bail to get out while waiting for a jurisdictional hearing or disposition. A jurisdictional hearing is the same thing as a trial in an adult court. Most juvenile courts use the word "disposition" instead

of "sentence." The judge decides whether
the adolescent must be locked up until
a jurisdictional hearing or disposition.
Only four states allow jury trials for
adolescents.

The Same Laws

Adolescents are prosecuted under the
same laws as adults and jail time is based
on the same penal codes used for adults.
The only differences are that most adolescents are not given the maximum penalty
for their crime and usually do their time in
a juvenile facility. Juvenile facilities, also
called juvenile hall, are county jails for
adolescents. State youth authorities are
penitentiaries for adolescents.

Juveniles can be tried as adults. Youths
under the age of 16 are assumed to be fit
for trial in juvenile court. If the district
attorney wants the case to be handled by
the adult court, he or she has to prove that
the youth is unfit to be tried in juvenile
court. If the youth is over 16, his defense
attorney must prove that the case is fit to
be handled by the juvenile court.

In either case, the juvenile court judge
makes the decision. This decision is based
on the severity of the crime, previous
crimes committed, and previous arrests.

Adolescent offenders are punished by the court under the same laws used for adults.

The laws in most states are being changed to make it easier for adolescents to be tried in adult courts. More adolescents are committing serious crimes, and more of them are being tried in adult courts.

Most crimes that lead to an adolescent's being tried in an adult court are crimes of violence. Those are crimes in which someone is killed, seriously injured, raped, or kidnapped, and in which a gun or other dangerous weapon is used. If the youth is caught selling, trafficking, preparing, or making a large amount of a drug, he or she can be tried in an adult court. Each case is looked at separately. If the teen is convicted in an adult court, he or she can be sentenced to an adult facility or to a juvenile facility.

Juvenile Penalties

Most adolescents are given several chances to get their act together, unless they have committed a serious crime. There are many programs to help young people get back on track. Charges can be dismissed if a youth gets counseling and does not commit another offense. For a first or second minor offense, the sentence may be a short stay in a juvenile detention facility and probation requiring counseling and

48 good behavior. Probation often requires random testing and drug-abuse counseling if drugs were involved in the crime. If the youth offends again or commits a serious crime, his time in juvenile hall increases and the probation rules become more strict. Most counties have work farms as a last step before sending a youth to a state youth authority.

In juvenile court, the word "petition" is used instead of "criminal charges." Drug selling is a felony. You don't have to be in possession of a large amount of drugs to be charged and convicted of drug sales. A teen can be charged with drug sales if he has a pager or a "pay/owe sheet" and a large amount of cash. A pay/owe sheet is a piece of paper or book with names and numbers of people owed or paid money. Young people who are found guilty of or admit to drug sales or trafficking petition receive much heavier penalties.

Many adolescents take advantage of the second chance they are given and do get back on track. Others laugh at the penalties and don't realize that things quickly get much worse. At first the penalties are less than those in an adult court because the court wants to help young people. Most judges realize that youths who commit crimes are often abused, neglected, or troubled and need help, not just punishment. If the teen continues to commit crimes, however, he can be treated like an adult criminal. He will receive a longer sentence and be sent to a state youth authority or in some cases, an adult jail or penitentiary.

Choosing to live without drugs means a happier and healthier life for you and those around you.

CHAPTER 5

Taking Action

*N*ow that you know more about the drug business, how it works, and many of the dangers involved, it's up to you to decide what to do about it.

Choices and Decisions

Sometimes it may seem as though drugs are your only road to wealth and freedom. Drug dealers may tempt you with visions of sports cars, fancy clothes, and lots of money. Gang members may offer you security and friendship. If you don't have people you can trust at home or at school, it may be harder to see another way of getting support from others.

52

But drug dealers and gang members don't tell you the whole story. They don't tell you that the people at the top make most of the money. They don't tell you that as a lookout, spotter, courier, dealer, or enforcer, you are at the greatest risk of being arrested or killed.

Drug dealers also don't tell you that if you start using your product, you run the risk of becoming addicted. Then you not only use up the drug you're supposed to sell, you also make the dealer unable to trust you to sell it. This will put your life at risk.

Over 1.3 million people were arrested for drug-related crimes in 1994. The average sentence length of those convicted of a drug-related crime was six and a half years.

There is no way to know how many people are killed every year because of drugs. The drug world is not a safe place. Unless you live long enough to become a drug lord or to become the head of an operation, the drug business will not make you rich. It is more likely to put you in jail or in the cemetery. The best thing for you to do is to stay away from the drug business.

Selling drugs may seem like an easy way to get rich. But there
are dangerous risks that a dealer must take.

Good Decisions

The first step toward helping yourself
stay away from the drug business is to
stay in school.

According to a 1992 survey done by
the California Attorney General's office,
one in three high school dropouts in
California is a member of a gang. And
most gangs are in some way connected
to the drug trade.

In July 1996, the Justice Department
reported that young people who drop out
of school are more likely to take drugs,

54 join gangs, and be victims of violent crime. The Justice Department has begun a nation-wide effort to keep teens in school.

National Efforts

In 1997, the U.S. government was granted a budget of over $16 billion to fight the war against drugs.

In 1996, President Bill Clinton began a grant program called "An Ounce of Prevention." This program gives money to community-based drug abuse prevention groups that are run by young people. A similar group may already be in your neighborhood. You can help that group by finding out more about the money available to help run it. For more information about applying for a grant, contact one of the organizations listed in the back of this book.

Seventy-five percent of all schools across the country participate in a program called Drug Abuse Resistance Education (DARE). This drug and violence prevention program is put together and run by teachers and police officers. It teaches students from kindergarten to twelfth grade the skills to resist drug use, violence, and gangs. Find out if this program is offered in your

school. If not, you can talk to your
teacher or guidance counselor and suggest
that your school join the program.

There has been a recent movement to
create "drug courts" that deal only with
drug crimes. The judge works with the
prosecutor, defender, and drug treatment
specialists to decide the best course of
treatment for a person convicted of
using or selling illegal drugs. Although
no one is sure how well drug courts are
working, some people believe that these
courts will help control the growing
number of drug crimes. The first drug
court began in Miami, Florida, in 1989.
Now they are in over twenty cities in the
United States.

Community Efforts

Many communities have programs to
fight drugs, alcohol, and gun violence in
their areas.

The Valley Partnership for Drug
Prevention, in Aspen, Colorado, sponsors
a program called Youth to Youth. Their
goal is to have students help each other
learn how to avoid drugs and the drug
business. Together, the teens create social
activities that don't involve drinking or
using drugs.

56   Many schools across the country run an organization called Teen Advisors. Teen Advisors make a year-long commitment to being drug, alcohol, and tobacco-free. The group works to make schools, homes, and communities safe and healthy places to be.

Ask your teacher or guidance counselor if your school offers programs or groups like these. If not, talk to them about how to start one.

Personal Efforts

You can help yourself and your community by learning about the dangers of the drug business, and talking about it with friends and family. Here are some suggestions on how you can learn more:

- Research. Learn about the drugs you have seen or heard about. Once you know more about these drugs, you can understand how they hurt not only the user, but the community as well.
- Spread knowledge. Share what you've learned about the dangers of drugs. Explain how they impact your community. Talk to others about drug-related issues. Call in to radio

shows that discuss youth issues.

- Promote a drug-free lifestyle. Throw a party that is drug and alcohol-free. Invite your friends and see how much fun you can have without drugs or alcohol.
- Join a sport, organization, or other activity. Sports teams are great places to make friends. Members of a group or team can help each other out in all kinds of situations.
- Get a part-time job. It's worth the effort. Not only will you make money, but you will also learn skills that you can use when you apply for full-time jobs.
- Raise community awareness about the problems, fears, and realities that teens in your area face. Talk to others about what's going on in your neighborhood.

By understanding the consequences of using or selling drugs, you can protect yourself from the dangers involved. You can also work with your community against the growing problem of drug use and drug-related crimes.

Glossary
Explaining New Words

accomplice Person who helps someone to plan or commit a crime.

addiction Inability to control the use of a drug.

admission Confessing to having done something.

advisor Person who gives advice or information.

chemist Person who runs an illegal drug-making operation.

clandestine Secret.

cook Person who makes illegal drugs.

cross To turn someone in to the police, or to rip someone off.

disposition The sentence or penalty in juvenile court.

felony Serious crime, usually punished by a prison term of more than one year.

front To give drugs to someone who will sell them and pay later.

hierarchy A system in which there are different levels of authority.

incarceration Putting a person in prison
   or other confinement.
jurisdictional hearing Trial in juvenile
   court.
money laundering Process that disguises
   illegal money as legal money. It is done
   by mixing drug money with the profits
   of a legal business and paying taxes
   on it.
penitentiary State or federal prison for
   serious offenders.
petition An indictment or complaint;
   charges.
pharmacologist Person who studies the
   effects of drugs on the body.
pig Person who tests an illegal drug.
pulling tricks Selling sex for money or
   drugs.
recruitment The act of persuading someone to join a group or organization.
rehabilitation Restoring a person to
   good health or behavior.
step on To mix a drug with similar-
   looking substances to increase its
   amount and the seller's profit. It is
   also called "cutting."
turned out Person who is addicted to
   drugs and trades sex for drugs.

Where to Go for Help

Alcoholics Anonymous
P.O. Box 459
Grand Central Station
New York, NY 10163
(212) 870-3400
Web site: http://www.
  alcoholics-
  anonymous.org/
e-mail: 76245-2153@
  compuserve.com

Children's Defense Fund
25 E Street NW
Washington, DC 20001
(202) 628-8787
Web site:
  http://www.tmn.com/
  cdf/index.html/
e-mail: cdfinfo@
  childrensdefense.org

Drug Abuse Resistance
  Education (DARE)
P.O. Box 512090
Los Angeles, CA 90051
(310) 215-0575
(800) 223-DARE
Web site http://dare-
  america.com/

Juvenile Justice
  Clearinghouse
Ounce of Prevention
  Program
P.O. Box 6000
Rockville, MD 20849
(301) 251-5500
(800) 638-8736
Web site: http://www.
  ncjrs.org/

Narcotics Anonymous (NA)
World Service Office
19737 Nordhoff Place
Chatsworth, CA 91311
(818) 773-9999
e-mail: wso@aol.com

The National
  Clearinghouse for
  Alcohol and Drug
  Information
P.O. Box 2345
Rockville, MD 20847
(301) 468-2600
(800) 729-6686
Web site: http://www.
  health.org/
e-mail: info@health.org

National Institute on
Drug Abuse
Public Information
Department
5600 Fisher Lane
Rockville, MD 20857
(301) 443-1124
(800) 662-HELP
Web site: http://www.
nida.nih.gov/
e-mail: information@
www.nida.nih.gov

In Canada:

Alcoholics Anonymous
#202 Intergroup Office
234 Ellington Avenue E
Toronto, ON M4P 1K5
(416) 487-5591

Crime Responsibility &
Youth
Suite 223
151-10090 152nd Street
Surrey, BC V3R 8X8
(800) CRY-1992
Web site: http://www2.
deepcove.com/cry/
e-mail: cry@deepcove.
com

Narcotics Anonymous
P.O. Box 7500
Station A
Toronto, ON M5W 1P9
(416) 691-9519

61

For Further Reading

Edwards, Gabrielle. *Drugs on Your Streets*. New York: Rosen Publishing Group, 1997.

Landow, Elaine. *Your Legal Rights*. New York: Walker, 1995.

McFarland, Rhoda. *Coping with Substance Abuse*. New York: Rosen Publishing Group, 1990.

Rosenberg, Maxine B. *On the Mend: Getting Away From Drugs*. New York: Maxwell Macmillan International, 1991.

Sexias, Judith S. *Drugs: What They Are and What They Do*. New York: William Morrow and Co., 1991.

Washburne, Carolyn Kott. *Drug Abuse*. San Diego, CA: Lucent Books, 1996.

Index

About the Author

Victor Adint has worked as a drug-abuse counselor and educator since 1986. He began working in outpatient and inpatient drug treatment and psychiatric facilities with adolescents, adults, and families. He went to work in an adult jail, where he developed and administrated one of the first comprehensive drug treatment programs for county jail facilities in the nation. He has been a drug and crime prevention consultant in Sacramento, California.

Photo Credits

Cover photo © Taylor-Frabricus/Gamma-Liaison; pp. 2, 15, 37, 41, 42 © AP/Wide World Photos; p. 9 © Naquen Producciones/Gamma-Liaison; p. 17 © Carlos Angel/ Gamma-Liaison; p. 18 © N. Utsumi/Gamma-Liaison; pp. 21, 50 by Stuart Rabinowitz; p. 22 © Susan Greenwood/ Gamma-Liaison; p. 25 Riha/Gamma-Liaison; p. 26 © John Berry/Gamma-Liaison; p. 30 © Doug Burrows/Gamma-Liaison; p. 32 © Ken Ross/Gamma-Liaison; p. 46 © Stephen Ferry/Gamma-Liaison; p.53 by John Novajosky.